# Unleash Your Values: How to Lead and Succeed in Business Today

## A Helicopter Pilot's Spin on Developing the Leader in You

## by Tom Crea

*Reggie,*
*Live Your Values!*
*All My Best,*
*Tom*

# Unleash Your Values: How to Lead and Succeed in Business Today - A Helicopter Pilot's Spin on Developing the Leader in You

Copyright 2016 by Tom Crea
All rights reserved worldwide.

Second Printing, 2016

ISBN 1532804962

Blackhawk Consulting Group, LLC
2400 Oxford Drive #122
Bethel Park, PA 15102
Printed by CreateSpace, an Amazon Company

Library of Congress Cataloging-in-Publication Data
Crea, Tom

## Unleash Your Values: How to Lead and Succeed in Business Today - A Helicopter Pilot's Spin on Developing the Leader in You

**Attention Corporations, Companies, Universities, Professional Organizations, and Trade Associations:** Quantity discounts are available on bulk purchases of this book. This book's Introduction can be customized for your organization to fit your specific needs. Contact Tom Crea at tom@blackhawkleader.com or 412.347.6151

# Dedication

To all those I served with, especially members of the 52ⁿᵈ Aviation Battalion, 2-17 Cavalry Squadron, and the Liberty Battalion (ROTC), as well as every past, present, and future military member. Thank you for living and sustaining our values-based culture; a special thanks to Colonel (Retired) Mike Pulliam, my first Battalion Commander, mentor, and role model.

# Table of Contents

# Introduction

The path to a leadership role varies. You might be a star performer promoted to management, a person inspired to take on a cause, or someone who chose to go through a formal leadership development program.

Either way, everyone is as an individual contributor, but to serve effectively as a leader, you need the right balance of interpersonal (people) and technical skills. With the shift in position comes a shift in the balance of skills required to do the job.

Although your company may not have told you when they offered you the promotion, managers need strong people skills to succeed. As an individual contributor, you likely did not receive interpersonal skills training as part of your leadership development.

In 1998, the Center for Creative Leadership concluded that 40 percent of new management hires fail within the first 18 months; 82 percent of the time, the reason was a failure to build good relationships. As recently as 2016, they continued to reach similar conclusions.

## The Skills Curve

Resource Associates Corporation uses the skills curve, depicted in the diagram below, which suggests that at the individual contributor level, 90 percent of your success depends upon your technical skills and only 10 percent depends on your people skills.

As soon as you get promoted to your first supervisory position it's 50/50, and that's where the greatest change occurs. Suddenly, 50 percent of your success is based on your technical skills, and 50 percent on your people skills.

You were identified for promotion to management because of your technical abilities, where you had previous training. Now, you have to apply a different set of skills.

- Will your management provide you the skills training and leadership development opportunities you will need to succeed?
-
- If not, how will you develop these skills on your own?

# ᵗʰᵉ**Skills Curve**

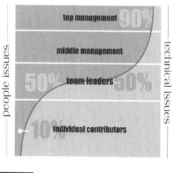

Take off to new possibilities!

After your promotion to supervisor or manager, the skills you need to succeed are much, much different. You become more dependent on other people and their abilities; you have to get along with them, get the most out of them, and get everyone to work together.

As you move to middle management, the ratio tips even more; 25 percent of your success is based on your technical and 75 percent on people skills.

Finally, in upper management, it's completely reversed; only 10 percent of your success is based on your technical competence, while 90 percent is based on people skills.

- How do you get everyone to hitch his or her horse to the same wagon and pull in the same direction?
- As you move further up the ladder, can you get teams of teams to work together?

## Personal Note

I truly believe that I had the privilege of learning leadership in the best possible environment in the world. Unlike many who find leadership positions stressful, I found every one of my opportunities enjoyable, a career that I would gladly repeat. I'd like you to feel the same.

I had the advantage of experiencing a proven leadership development process when I started in ROTC. For those four years and my first six years in the Army, I continued to gain practical experience in various leadership roles, where I had the chance to learn, apply, and refine my interpersonal (people) skills. When I received my first command assignment, I had a distinct advantage.

The leadership development process never stopped. And, at the end of my career, I was running an Army ROTC leadership development program at two Boston schools: Northeastern University and Boston College, similar to where I started.

In this book, I share valuable lessons learned from personal experience, stories that parallel many of the leadership challenges you have, or will have. My purpose is to get you thinking about what matters most: your values, those of the company you work for, and aligning the two.

By offering critical leadership challenges to consider before you reach any forks in the road, my hope is that you'll be better prepared when moments of decision arise.

If you are just beginning your career as a manager and have questions about leadership, this book is for you. If you have been a leader and are moving into middle management, this book is for you. And, if you are the owner of a company or a senior leader looking to inspire your leadership team, this book is for you.

Once you've walked through these pages with me, you will understand what it means to Define & Align, Lead & Succeed, Instill & Fulfill, Relate & Communicate, and, Discover Your Inner Gyroscope, what keeps you at operating speed so that you are balanced, stable, and continue to head in the right direction.

## In the Next Chapter...

...we'll explore what **values** mean to you and your team.  I'll present examples of how your values and beliefs can be tested, and what it means to **align your values with your company's values**.

# Chapter 1

# 1. Define & Align

Why do we join organizations or participate in certain events? With so many different opportunities available these days, what attracts each of us to a variety of possibilities?

Imagine that you are a gifted athlete, capable of playing any professional sport. You decide upon baseball.

- What attracted you to baseball?

You enjoy playing the game. But, you could have played soccer, or basketball, or another sport. The main reason you chose baseball is that you would rather spend your time in this environment. It was the culture, and at its heart, its values, that attracted you.

When people feel that they are in a place where company values match their own, they feel aligned, and that is what attracts, and ultimately retains people to an organization.

## Was I in the Right Place?

When I joined the Army, my goal was to be a General Officer. I went through ROTC, bought into the culture, and believed I was in the right place.

At my basic training course, we progressed from land navigation on foot at 3 km/hr to 30 km/hr in the M113 Armored Personnel Carrier (similar to a tank), 10 times faster than I was used to – and I was challenged!

While licking my wounds that weekend, my roommate walks in and sees me reading Dale Carnegie's, *How to Win Friends and Influence People.* He blurts out:

> "Why are you reading THAT book? You don't need to read that, you're going to be the boss."

I was shocked and started to wonder whether this was the environment I wanted: Was I in the right place?

A month later, I was in flight school. Again, at the end of the 9-month course: navigation. Now, our speed was 150 km/h, 50 times faster than when I was last successful. I had the same challenge, and the same experience. I needed practice.

Here is how I learned I was in the right place.

## Setting

In the Army, every commissioned officer outranks every warrant officer, and every warrant officer outranks every non-commissioned officer.

After 13 months of schools, I arrived at my first unit, where I was given a platoon leader role. My platoon included an instructor pilot and a platoon sergeant, each with 10 or more years of experience than I.

The moment I entered the Army, I outranked them both; an interesting dynamic and challenge for every young leader!

## 12 Hours Bottle to Throttle

In October 1984 at K-16 Air Base, just south of Seoul, Korea, one of my early opportunities to fly came on a Saturday morning. I was a brand new pilot, officer, and platoon leader, less than three months in my new position, and eager to fly. I needed to get flight time and experience; I wanted to fix my navigation weakness.

As I returned from my helicopter pre-flight, Mr. Welda (my instructor pilot) told me that he smelled alcohol on Sergeant X (our crew chief); this violated our "12-hour, bottle to throttle" rule. Sergeant X was older than I was, and he had more than 6 years in the Army. Despite my youth and inexperience, Sergeant X worked for me. It was up to me to take action – but I had no clue what to do.

Mr. Welda: Sir, you should take Sergeant X in for a drug and alcohol test.

Me: *(I was concerned because Sergeant X had a wife and family and I didn't think things would go well for him; my hesitation showed.)*

Mr. Welda: Sir, you need to take him in.

All I wanted to do that Saturday was fly, not answer the underlying question of whether I was committed to the Army's values or our aviation policies. Instead of flying, I found myself escorting my sergeant to the nearest medical facility.

After we returned, I spent the rest of the weekend wondering: What will my boss think? More important, what will SFC Watson, my platoon sergeant, the one who is training me, teaching me the ropes, think? I liked our relationship. What about the rest of my platoon... the rest of the unit?

Monday morning, I reported to my commander, Major Vivolo.

Me: *(Knees shaking, I explained what happened.)*

Major Vivolo: Tom, I'm just tickled pink that you had the gumption to do the right thing and take him in.

Me: *(Hmmm. Maybe, I did the right thing.)*

Next, I went behind closed doors with my platoon sergeant.

SFC Watson: Sir, I didn't like what you did to Sergeant X on Saturday, but you did the right thing, and I'm going to support you.

All the tension from the weekend finally left my body! I was in the right place. This was the environment for me. My values were aligned with the Army's values.

## Values and Beliefs

Let's revisit our gifted athlete scenario. By making the choice to play baseball, you subconsciously feel that this is the right place for you. You feel like you can pursue your goals and dreams while living your values within a supportive environment; you are ready to perform.

- Beliefs – things you hold to be true
- Values -- principles or beliefs that you consider worthwhile; those that should guide your actions

## Core Values

An organization's values and beliefs are the magnet that attracts the right talent to their culture. From day one and throughout my career, the Army made clear its values, those that would define our culture, represented by the acronym LDRSHIP:

- Loyalty - *Bear true faith and allegiance to the U.S. Constitution, the Army, your unit, and other Soldiers*
- Duty - *Fulfill your obligations*

- Respect - *Treat people as they should be treated*
- Selfless Service - *Put the welfare of the Nation, the Army, and subordinates before your own*
- Honor - *Live up to all the Army Values*
- Integrity - *Do what's right—legally and morally*
- Personal Courage - *Face fear, danger, or adversity (physical and moral)*

*-- FM 6-22: Army Leadership*

These values resonated with me.

We also learned the 4 Cs of leadership:

- Courage - *action in the face of fear; stepping up to the danger with a clear purpose*
- Candor - *the ability to show openness, concern, and honesty*
- Competence - *obtaining the knowledge and skills necessary to perform a task or obtain a goal*
- Commitment - *acting on promises regardless of personal difficulty and sacrifice*

Similar to every other organization, our professed set of values and beliefs attracted a certain segment of the population, where every new member had a good idea of the culture they were joining.

Values from company to company will be different, but whether you choose to follow these values and support your culture will be the same.

In my example, I was fortunate to be in an incredibly supportive environment with three distinct groups of professionals dedicated to developing young leaders like me.

Let's revisit how an organization defines its values and how the people within create the culture.

Mr. Welda, a warrant officer and my instructor pilot, advised me and pointed me in the right direction.

Major Vivolo, a commissioned officer and my commanding officer, backed my decision.

And, SFC Watson, a non-commissioned officer and my platoon sergeant, supported me by upholding the standard. He continued to be a fantastic advisor and mentor in the months that followed.

Three men from three career paths put to rest the doubt in my mind from my encounter with my roommate at my basic course. Through their actions, they helped me reach an extremely important decision. They validated my career choice. More important, they solidified my commitment to the Army's culture.

As a business example, some notable corporate comments from the Wells Fargo website address the following about values:

"Our values should guide every conversation, decision, and interaction."

"If we can't link what we do to one of our values, we should ask ourselves why we're doing it. It's that simple."

"Corporate America is littered with the debris of companies that crafted lofty values on paper but, when put to the test, failed to live by them. We believe in values lived, not phrases memorized. If we had to choose, we'd rather have a team member who lives by our values than one who just memorizes them."

## Keys to Your Leadership Success

- Recruiting: If you build it (a values-based organization), they will come; what your company markets.

- Retention: If you practice them (your organizational values), they will stay; what your company lives.

## Business Insight

Values are the heart of what attracts and retains people to your organization. When people feel they are in a place where their company values match their own, they feel aligned. They are more committed, happier, and more productive; the essence of great teams.

## Promoting Your Culture

You chose to play baseball. When you entered this sport, you implicitly agreed to support its values and promote the culture. And, when you signed with your team, you made the same commitment to your organization.

- Culture – the set of values and beliefs that define a community; inherited from predecessors, lived today, and passed on to those who will follow.

Everyone wants to fit in where the company values align with his or her own. This also implies that each member has a responsibility to uphold the culture, its values, and its traditions; especially leaders.

> *There is an expression: Culture eats strategy for breakfast.*

### A Test of Commitment

The day I accepted my commission as an Army officer, I swore an oath to uphold the Army's values. Sixteen months later, I had an important obligation to fulfill them. Unpleasant as it was that Saturday morning, I owed it to everyone who subscribed to our culture to hold Sergeant X accountable.

Three officers taught me that if I wanted to be a part of the culture, I had to do my part. As a leader, I was expected to uphold the Army values. Despite my youth and inexperience, I had a duty to fulfill.

Imagine if I did not believe in the Army's values.

- Would I have chosen to protect Sergeant X's career instead?
- If so, what message would I have sent to everyone else?
- And, how would that support those who signed on to the culture?

**I would not have been aligned.**

## Keys to Your Leadership Success

- I discovered that real power comes from your ability to influence. Mr. Welda taught me that lesson through his knowledge, advice, and support. I just had to be willing to listen.

- Leadership means you have a responsibility to do the right thing. If you don't know the answers, you have to know where to find them.

- Everyone wants to fit in where the company values align with his or her own. As a leader, you have to make everyone feel that they made the right choice and they are in the right place.

- Make sure your values are aligned with your industry, and your corporate culture.

## Business Insights

Being a leader has enough challenges when you are committed to your organization. When you are in a position of authority, you have a responsibility to uphold the culture, its values, and its traditions. Leadership is about much more than position. Don't make it unnecessarily hard by attempting to lead in an organization where you don't believe in its values. Your personal and professional values must align.

*Your organization decides its values; the membership creates the culture.*

### Find a Role Model, Mentor, or Coach

In the Introduction, I stated that it was my privilege to learn leadership in the Army. In the story I shared, different members supported the culture through their actions, their behavior.

Leadership is critical to sustain these traditions, and once again, I felt privileged that my first battalion commander was a fantastic role model. In my first two years, Lieutenant Colonel Mike Pulliam taught me a number of lessons.

For example, he taught me that when leaders show they care about others, people appreciate it and they respond. Here are just a couple of lessons I learned from Mike, as simple as remembering names and instilling loyalty.

## The Importance of People

Mike appreciated others and it showed. He treated people well and his interest was genuine. Despite his seemingly vast responsibilities and the constant 8% monthly personnel turnover involved with one year rotating assignments, he made the effort to learn our names.

Mike was in charge of a battalion of 700+ soldiers dispersed among four companies geographically hours apart. I had just come from the largest, a company of about 250 people, where I felt that I "knew" most of the members of my old unit.

Shortly after I began working on Mike's staff, we paid my old company a visit. As we walked through the base, he greeted people as we went — by name, every one of them. I was embarrassed that he knew more people in my old unit than I did, and I had seen them daily for the last ten months!

When we visited the other units, Mike did this again and again, causing me to wonder: how was it possible he could remember so many names?

When I had the opportunity to ask him his secret, I learned one of the most valuable lessons of my career. He told me it was as simple as consciously remembering something about each person. At first, he had to practice. After a while, it just came to him naturally.

## Keys to Your Leadership Success

- Names are important to everyone; remember them.

- Pronounce names properly; it is a sign of respect.

## Business Insights

When leaders make an effort to learn names, they show that they care about others; people appreciate it and they respond.

## Loyalty Starts with You

On another occasion, a peer had made a poor decision that gained unwanted attention from Mike's boss. The next thing we heard about his poor decision was... absolutely nothing. We wondered why the bad news did not, let's say, roll downhill.

It wasn't until later that we learned Mike had taken the heat. As our leader, he believed it was his responsibility to provide guidance and develop his team. This meant allowing us room to make mistakes. He believed that if we could choose, we would do the right thing.

- How do you think this made us feel?

We all felt empowered. We had great respect for Mike and we felt that we let him down. His actions firmed our resolve to work harder and to never let this happen again. He taught us that loyalty was part of leadership. As a consequence, his soldiers would follow him anywhere.

### Keys to Your Leadership Success

- Provide an environment where your team can learn and grow.

- Accept responsibility for the actions of every member of your unit.

### Business Insights

Set the example. If you want to instill loyalty or any other leadership trait in your employees, you need to demonstrate the trait first.

## Why You Want to Act

Imagine yourself, a new employee, just out of school or training, eager to apply what you learned. You enter your new organization and you want to see how you will fit in: Did you make the right career choice? Does this community live their professed values?

- You deserve to work in the environment you signed up for, don't you?

Employee happiness and organizational performance are a predictable outcome of good leadership. When the leader upholds the company's values and culture, employees are more motivated and productive.

- They too, deserve to work in the culture they signed up for, don't they?

This is where you, the leader, come in. Perhaps more than any other factor, your success, and happiness, depend on whether you are in the right culture and you do your part and live the company values.

I was fortunate to cut my teeth as I started my career under Mike Pulliam's leadership.

Beliefs matter because they represent your convictions. Values represent your deepest beliefs.

# Define & Align

*It is much, much easier to lead when you are committed to the culture and aligned with your company's values and beliefs.*

## Steps for the *Leader* to Apply

1. **Assess your goals, using your personal values and beliefs to guide your choices.**

   a. Identify your personal goals in these six categories: mental, physical, social, spiritual, family, and financial.

   b. What percentage of your time do you want to spend in each area (ideal)? This will help you determine what you value most, your long-term goals if you will, and get you started.

   c. Spend a month tracking your time. Where did you spend your time (actual)? Compare your ideal percentages to your actual time.

   d. Determine what you'd like to change. In order to progress from where you actually spend your time to what you really want, you'll need to make some changes. This means learning to say "no" to those things that take you away from your goals and the things you value. Spend your time so that it becomes aligned with your goals.

   e. Download my Time Tracker spreadsheet to help you accomplish the above, available here:
   http://info.blackhawkleader.com/define-and-align-time-tracker-lp

2. **Are you aligned?**

   a. To lead effectively, review your company values. Your employees have done this and they are expecting you to uphold the culture.

   b. Get familiar with the values of other organizations. For instance, download FM 6-22, *Army Leadership,* to discover the values so important to the Army culture (free here: http://armypubs.army.mil/doctrine/DR_p ubs/dr_a/pdf/fm6_22.pdf).

   c. The goal is to see how different values attract different groups of people and realize *what motivates* others to join your culture.

3. **Commit.** Decide whether you can support your company culture fully so that you uphold its values and beliefs.

   a. Again, assess your values and beliefs.

   b. When your values align with your company's values, you'll be more committed, happier… and, more productive.

   c. Remember that the same values that attracted you attracted others as well. As a leader, you are responsible to live these values and maintain your culture.

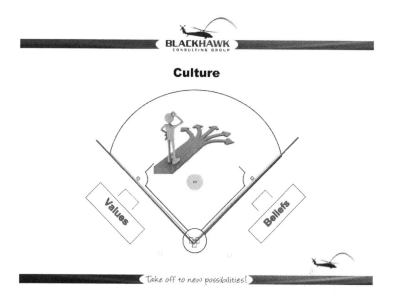

**Culture**

When you chose baseball, the ball field's boundaries represented your values and beliefs.

Use your boundaries to guide your decisions and keep you and your team heading toward your most important goals.

Here's a graphic and definition of employee engagement from MacLeod & Clarke that will help you achieve alignment:

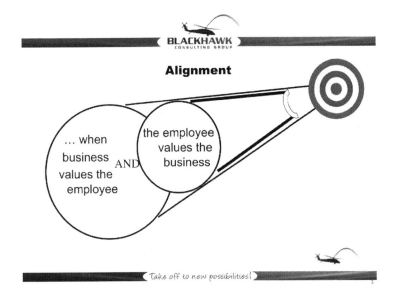

Take off to new possibilities!

## 4. To go deeper, I recommend:

a) Read Stephen Covey's classic, *The 7 Habits of Highly Effective People.* Note: Instead of six categories mentioned in 1 a, Covey uses four.

b) Read *Nuts: Southwest Airline's Crazy Recipe for Business and Personal Success,* by Kevin & Jackie Freiberg.

c) Increase your self-awareness and discover your strengths, blind spots, and potential weak areas regarding your decision-making style, motivators, and communication preferences. Take the comprehensive, 3-part ADVanced Insights™ assessment, available here: blackhawkleader.com/leadership-assessment-tools/

# Values Notes

## In the Next Chapter...

... we'll explore how self-awareness is the basis for leadership via: **presence, intellect, and character,** or the **Army's BE-KNOW-DO motto.**

Also, we'll differentiate:
- **Authority and Responsibility**
- **Power and Authority**

And continue to see how **values alignment** is a predictor of every leader's happiness and success.

# Chapter 2

# 2. Lead & Succeed

Good leadership begins with one critical component: self-awareness. The Army instilled in us its BE-KNOW-DO motto, that is, we should evaluate and strive to improve in three areas, continuously; our presence, intellect, and character.

By focusing on the fundamentals that follow, you'll inspire the trust and confidence that leads to aligned teams.

## Presence and Character  (BE and DO)

In *Grounded*, Bob Rosen describes the heart of the Army's Be-Know-Do motto by explaining the difference between presence (BE) and character (DO) with a great tree metaphor.

He suggests that your actions, which represent your character (DO), are on display just as the branches and leaves of a tree are on display. But, not on display, not visible to others, are your roots, and they are the essence that defines who you are, your presence (BE).

- Did you know that there are more than a dozen ingredients in the soil that plants need to be healthy?

Like a tree needs fertile ground to grow, leaders need to prepare the soil to nurture a healthy root system. The best way for me to share the impact is via this parable from the New Testament:

> The sower went out to sow and as he sowed some seed that fell on the path and the birds came and ate it up. Other seed fell on rocky ground where it had little soil. It sprang up at once because the soil was not deep. And when the sun rose it scorched and withered it for lack of roots. Some seed fell among thorns and the thorns grew up and choked it and it produced no grain. And some seed fell on *rich soil* and it produced fruit. It came up and grew and yielded 30, 60, 100-fold.

## *Focus on what others can't see – develop your roots.*

## How?

I shared with you my story of Sergeant X. As a 23-year-old, I can assure you I had never made such an important decision in my life. Values alignment made this possible. When I considered the values my parents taught me along with the oath I swore at my commissioning ceremony, it was a matter of honor.

Like you, we learn our values from our parents or other influential people in our lives. At some point, we decide to make these values our own, or we have to choose a different set of values.

Sometimes, we don't realize our convictions or how much we are committed to our values until we are faced with our most difficult decisions.

### Keys to Your Leadership Success

- Character (DO) gets down to whether you are able to consistently do the right thing, especially during times of adversity.

- Spend time reflecting on the things that are important to you, the things that have meaning to you. When you face a tough choice, these are the ones that you won't compromise.

**Business Insights**

In the end, your actions define your character. While character is about what you DO, it is a reflection of your values. Spend your time nurturing your roots so that you develop your presence. (BE)

*"If you don't stick to your values when they're being tested, They're not values: they're hobbies."*
*- Jon Stewart*

## Authority and Responsibility

Learn to delegate! You'll empower others, make your team more successful, and at the same time, you'll demonstrate your potential for increased responsibilities.

Revisiting my "bottle to throttle" story with Sergeant X prompts an important question:

- What is the difference between authority and responsibility?

In that scenario, I had both authority and responsibility. In this scenario three years later, I had an experience that illustrates the difference more clearly.

- Authority: the power to enforce rules or give orders, a *privilege* given to an individual in a management or supervisory position.

- Responsibility: a duty or obligation where someone is held accountable.

## It's My Sister's Wedding!

In Army Aviation, pilots want to fly and the operations officer is the one in charge of the flight schedule. I had just been promoted to captain and I was serving my second Army Aviation assignment in the Republic of Korea.

I had been there a few months already, and as luck would have it, the operations officer slot I wanted in our 150-member organization opened up. There was a senior captain ahead of me, so he was assigned this coveted position I'd have another shot, but that meant I had to agree to extend my stay in Korea another seven months, which I did.

Not long after I became the operations officer our new commander arrived. When he called me into his office for our first meeting, he told me that my previously approved vacation request to attend my sister's wedding back in the U.S. was too close to our annual organizational evaluation.

He informed me that it was too important to have his operations officer away this close to such a key event. Then, he canceled my request.

Needless to say, I was not happy when I walked out of his office. It was my sister's wedding! Fortunately, I had some time to change his mind. That's when I first truly understood what it meant to delegate authority while maintaining responsibility.

## Learn to Delegate

The two operations officers before me handled flight scheduling personally. While I did this for a short time, I felt that I had grasped all of the nuances and intricacies involved, so I decided to delegate this task to one of my very capable officers.

Inevitably, when it came to the flight schedule, platoon leaders would barter for more flight time for *their* pilots. I know I did. However, just like my predecessors, the operations officer typically outranked the platoon leaders, so he or she could easily end any debate.

My flight-scheduling officer, Tom Sylvia, was a sharp warrant officer and pilot. He was more than capable of handling flight scheduling equitably, but as I indicated earlier, commissioned officers outrank warrant officers.

I made clear that these were now Tom's decisions; I had full confidence in him and it would take something extraordinary for me to intervene.

For the first several weeks, there were challenges and attempts to have me to overrule one of Tom's decisions. I didn't bite.

Instead, I continually redirected comments and reinforced that I had given Tom full authority. It didn't take long for everyone to adapt. I had delegated my authority and Tom was in charge.

In the end, I was able to persuade my commander to change his mind and attend my sister's wedding because:

- As Mike Pulliam taught us, I made clear that I was responsible for Tom's performance
- Tom was doing a fantastic job

Deciding to delegate was a light bulb moment for me; it transformed how I would lead throughout my career.

I discovered that if I could let go of a role so coveted, I could learn to let go and delegate whenever I found someone else who was willing and capable. If they were willing and ready like Tom, the decision was easy.

Later, I learned that if they were not ready, but willing, I'd make it a point to invest the time and train them until they were ready.

## Keys to Your Leadership Success

When you delegate:

- Avoid attempts to take charge so that others have the opportunity to learn and grow.

- Empower others to handle their responsibilities without your involvement by giving your full support.

- In the event of failure, determine whether you failed with your guidance, or the person exceeded his or her authority.

- In every instance, maintain responsibility.

## Business Insights

Army Axiom:
You can delegate authority, but you can never, ever, delegate responsibility.

## Power and Authority

Delegating enables others the opportunity to shine while freeing you to focus your attention where it is needed most. When you instill this attitude within the culture, you increase your ability to influence exponentially.

My previous examples bring up another important question:

- What is the difference between power and authority?

Let's start with definitions again, and then I want to share a story that illustrates this difference more clearly.

- Power: the capacity to change the actions, behavior, or opinions of others.

- Authority: the power to enforce rules or give orders, a privilege given to an individual in a management or supervisory position.

## Taking Command

After I departed South Korea the second time I was assigned to Fort Campbell, KY. A couple of months after I arrived, I received my first Army command where I was given complete responsibility for the health, welfare, and morale of 50 soldiers. We maintained and operated 13 Blackhawk helicopters in order to perform each of our assigned missions.

Our mission set was unique; I considered it the most diverse among 26 of my peers in the 101st Airborne Division. Instead of my pilots conducting multi-ship helicopter operations led by a single air mission commander, we needed every aircrew to be capable of performing any of our diverse, single-ship missions.

For example, my unit maintained two unique aircraft: those equipped with a Command and Control set of radios, and another set designed for Electronic Warfare. In both cases, my pilots deployed on individual flight plans to support the most senior leaders in the division.

Since each aircrew had to be able to operate independently on these high visibility missions, we had to develop the leadership skills of every pilot. At one point, I remember seven helicopters spread across seven different states.

## Instilling Responsibility in Others

To further complicate matters, our 2000-person Aviation Brigade was undergoing a reorganization effort. My unit became the focal point for a massive helicopter swap, where we exchanged 10 helicopters with 9 independent organizations. Each trade required an intensive airframe inspection to ensure the satisfaction of both parties; swaps that involved very detailed record keeping.

This was a massive undertaking, and simply put, not my strength. But again, I had someone who was willing and able to manage this task, so I delegated oversight to Warrant Officer Mike Bailey and let him run with it. He excelled. I stayed involved and maintained overall responsibility, but Mike handled all of the details.

I was glad that I had discovered the value of delegating during my operations officer role in Korea, because this time, I was pushed. Beyond the reorganization effort, I had to instill a sense of responsibility in every pilot because every one of them could be operating independent of their platoon leader or me.

This meant that I had to train my platoon leaders to delegate as well so that they could help me divide and conquer, if you will. But, I was short one key leader and after more than a year, I finally welcomed my third platoon leader. He arrived several months prior to a major, month-long exercise that we were going to participate in at the National Training Center (NTC).

## Responsibility, Power, and Authority

Our next field training exercise was going to be a perfect opportunity to observe and develop Zach Maner, my new platoon leader. After we setup base on a soggy cornfield in southeast Indiana about 50 miles northwest of Fort Campbell, we started to receive our missions.

I told Zach that he was going to be in charge, responsible for all of the planning and execution, but to keep me informed along the way. I paired him with Geary Powers, a warrant officer, and an experienced pilot. When the first mission came in, I sent Zach to the operations tent to get started.

Major Quinlan, our squadron operations officer who was senior to me, was concerned because he thought I needed to be more involved. This led to an unplanned visit from my boss, the squadron commander, Lieutenant Colonel Ruth.

> LTC Ruth: Tom, Major Q. is concerned that you're not involved.
>
> Me: Sir, this is a training exercise. This is my opportunity to observe and train Zach.
>
> LTC Ruth: Tom, yes, but it's a training exercise for the unit we support too. If you fail, they won't be able to train their unit.
>
> Me: Sir, I am still involved. I'm monitoring this every step of the way.
>
> LTC Ruth: Tom, I'm inclined to agree with Major Q.
>
> Me: Sir, I understand, but you know my mission better than anyone. I can't be in two places at once. I need to know whether I can count on Zach to lead on his own before we go to the NTC in three months.
>
> LTC Ruth: (still uncomfortable)

Me: Sir, I'm still responsible. I'd like your support.

LTC Ruth: OK Tom, we'll try it your way, but you're responsible!

Me: Yes, sir.

Meanwhile, I had not heard from Zach, so I strolled through the recently tilled, muddy cornfield. When I reached his tent, I asked him to come outside and give me an update. Zach proceeded to share what he knew about our first mission)

> Me: What about A, B, and C? Go back and get those answers. And this time, be sure you come and tell me without me having to find you.

Time passed and I didn't hear from Zach. Drizzle became rain. I donned my parka and trudged over to his tent and asked him to come out a second time.

> Me: I thought you were going to find me and give me an update?
>
> Zach: (no response)
>
> Me: What did you learn?
>
> Zach: (Proudly proceeds to share his increased understanding of our mission.)
>
> Me: Yes, but how will you do X, Y, and Z?
>
> Zach: (frustrated) I don't know, sir.

Me: Why not?

Zach: *(very frustrated)* No excuse, sir.

*(As part of the education process and the ever-important message the Army wanted to convey about accepting responsibility, officers learn as cadets that there are a limited number of acceptable responses. Here are three: Yes, sir. No, sir. No excuse, sir.)*

Me: OK Zach, let's cut the B.S. Why do you think I paired you with Geary?

Zach: *(still frustrated)* I don't know, sir.

Me: ***So you can learn!*** What makes you think that with your two months of experience that you know how to do this? I don't expect you to have all of the answers, but I do expect you to be big enough to ask for help know when you don't. This time, take Geary with you and have him teach you how we do this mission.

Zach: Yes, sir.

Zach and Geary led that mission, and the next, and the next successfully, and I avoided an unpleasant follow-on conversation with my boss!

That exercise was a **transformational experience** for me. I discovered how to delegate at a deeper level and develop my platoon leader at the same time, all via Geary. This is when I learned that

## *I enjoyed developing others more than I enjoyed flying helicopters.*

Perhaps more important, it was a transformational experience for Zach as well. Less than a year after our NTC rotation, I departed the unit while Zach went on to lead his platoon very ably during the first Iraq War.

## Keys to Your Leadership Success

- As much as possible, delegate authority and leverage the strengths *(power)* of others. Let them shine and help you build your team.

- Place your focus on developing others.

- Free yourself so that you are able to turn your attention to where it is needed most.

## Business Insights

"Leaders don't create followers, they create more leaders."

-- Tom Peters

## Why You Want to Act

You are in charge, so you have the greatest ability to determine your team's destiny. You know that you do not have all of the answers and are willing to admit it. So, you reach out to others for help, give them credit for successes, and take the blame when things go wrong. After all, you're in charge.

Leadership starts with confidence in your values and beliefs. It is the basis for inspiring trust and confidence. It includes self-awareness, knowing who you are, and being comfortable in your role.

Without self-awareness, you won't be able to let go and delegate authority to others. This is a critical step to master before your responsibilities increase. Without self-awareness, it's also hard to demonstrate to senior management that you have the capacity to take on these positions of increased authority.

To recap, there are steps you can take that will help you focus on strengthening your roots:

- Maintain your values and alignment
- Continuously seek self-improvement
- Foremost, develop your presence, part of your BE, KNOW, DO
- Ask for help when you need it
- Delegate authority while retaining responsibility

Learn to inspire others; each of the above will help you on your way.

# Lead & Succeed

## Steps for the *Leader* to Apply

1. **Alignment.** A good to way to check your values alignment and develop your presence (BE) is to complete a personal and a leadership wheel. As you can see below, there will be variations of shading depending on how well you are satisfied in each of these 10 areas. Check out https://youtu.be/S4qjgdhKM6c to learn how to complete this exercise and shade your personal and leadership wheels.

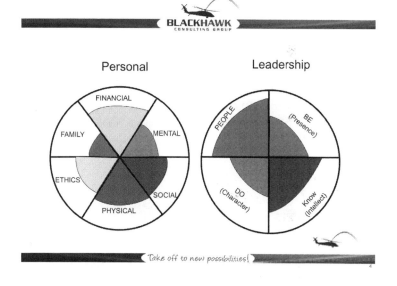

2. **Assess your leadership presence, intellect, and character** by evaluating your leadership goals in these four categories (refer to FM 6-22, *Army Leadership*ᴌ

   http://armypubs.army.mil/doctrine/DR_pubs/d r_a/pdf/fm6_22.pdf (for BE-KNOW-DO)

BE – Chapter 5

KNOW – Chapter 6

DO – Chapter 4

Interpersonal (People) Skills – See chapter 4 of this book.

3. **To go deeper, I recommend the following as well:**

a. Read one of my favorites, *The One-Minute Manager,* by Kenneth Blanchard and Spencer Johnson. This quick read clearly illustrates these basic leadership principles: the value of setting goals, what you need to do to reinforce the desired behavior (praise); and how to correct undesired behavior (reprimand).

b. Explore your decision-making strengths, blind spots, and potential weak areas identified in your results from the Attribute-Index portion of your 3-part ADVanced Insights™ assessment from Chapter 1.

# Personal Wheel Notes

## Leadership Wheel Notes

## In the Next Chapter...

...we'll explore why **teamwork** is essential, then address the building blocks for strong teams: individual development, team building, and how critical **values alignment** is to keeping everyone heading in the same direction.

# Chapter 3

# 3. Instill & Fulfill

**Teamwork** is a test of your ability to instill desire in others and leave them fulfilled. And, team building requires excellent **communication** skills on your part, as well as good communication within your team as well.

Too often, silos exist within organizations. Maybe marketing isn't communicating with sales, or neither department interacts well with operations.

Since teamwork is essential for the success of every organization, the existence of silos highlights the importance of taking advantage of every opportunity for the team to grow together so that you learn to rely on each other.

High performing organizations emphasize teamwork, and consequently, they consistently perform better than their competitors.

## A Life or Death Scenario: Teamwork is the Difference

Sometimes, your very survival depends upon your ability to operate as a team. Consider the raid to capture Osama bin Laden, which we'll explore later in this chapter.

Now, imagine another goal larger in scale, an air assault operation where an infantry unit of 200 men must attack an objective in a remote mountainous area. To get there, they must travel by helicopter and to increase safety, the operation must be done at night. Since it is a mountainous area, there isn't much open space; five helicopters are the most that can safely fit into the one landing zone (LZ) available.

Let's say each helicopter can carry 10 passengers, so this means the operation will need 20 aircraft to insert these troops. The infantry unit will have to be divided into four groups and they will arrive in the LZ in waves of 50 people each.

To increase their chances of survival, the four groups of infantry soldiers must arrive as quickly as possible, one after the other. Upon arrival, they will need to clear the LZ and then form a perimeter to provide security and allow the next group to land safely.

The helicopter unit will have to time its flights so that they land within 30 seconds of their scheduled arrival time, offload the troops, and then clear the area for the next flight of aircraft.

Finally, an Air Force organization will need to provide close air support aircraft to protect the flights of helicopters as well as the soldiers who are on the ground.

The complexity and various organizations involved require leadership, teamwork, and excellent communication skills from each, along with coordination and cooperation with one another.

## Synchronizing Three Team Missions

Imagine now that you are the leader of any one of these missions.

Each infantry member must know how to safely enter and exit the helicopter, and once it lands, know exactly where to go and what to do when they get there.

Each helicopter crew will have primary and secondary responsibilities such as flight navigation, coordination with the infantry unit, or coordination with close air support from supporting aircraft.

The close air support aircraft will need to be aware of the helicopter flight routes and the location of the infantry soldiers so that there are no friendly fire casualties.

Three separate organizations must coordinate missions, synchronize their efforts, and work as a team. So far, our scenario assumes everything will go as planned, but:

-   What if something goes wrong?

- How will your team react to unexpected events?
- Do you have contingency plans?

Whether your mission is simple or complex like the one described here, great teams are made up of confident, competent individuals who develop and gel into cohesive teams. Teamwork is the difference. So, how does a leader develop teamwork?

- What if people's values aren't aligned?

## Developing Competent Individuals

In order to build your team, you have to set the example by continuously improving yourself while you develop others.

When you consider basic wants and needs, people want to be treated with dignity and respect, and they want to be able to learn and grow. When you invest time in developing everyone on your team, each member grows and your performance improves exponentially.

Deep down, every employee wants to know how he or she will be treated individually, and, as a part of the team. Those answers depend on your organization's culture, and whether you create an environment that upholds your company's values.

From the time I started in ROTC, senior officers continually shared that our company command assignment would be the most cherished position during our military career. They were right.

A command position is a unique assignment, a combination of responsibility and authority where our society extends a sacred trust to its military leaders.

For this privilege, we are held responsible for the health and welfare of our soldiers, on and off duty. We are accountable for their training, growth, and development.

The effort you place into fundamentals, such as developing your people, is critical to every business. Ultimately, your success depends upon the environment you create.

## Be a Teacher, a Coach, a Mentor

Every employee craves feedback and every leader can find opportunities to train, coach, or mentor. The questions for you: Will you see those opportunities? How will you handle them as they arise?

In the last chapter on leadership, in the story that shaped my relationship with Zach, I provided an example that illustrated the power you have when you delegate authority to those that are capable. Now, I'll share another coaching opportunity that I had during meetings with Zach and his fellow platoon leaders, Bob Cockrell and Ed Touchet.

Equipment readiness is a big deal in the military. This is no different from the equipment used on a manufacturing assembly line. If the equipment is not ready, it hampers production. If your equipment isn't available for use, you're not ready.

In our case, we primarily operated 13 helicopters, which the Army expected us to maintain so that our airframe monthly readiness rate was at least 80% available. We had 10 UH-60A Blackhawk helicopters, and due to our process of always having one in phased maintenance, we could have no more than 9 available or do better than 90%.

Our phased maintenance program was non-negotiable, a standard part of our business process. Simply put, it was important for safety and extending the life of each airframe. It was something every commander and his or her subordinate platoon leaders had to manage.

## Competing Demands

In addition to their leadership responsibilities, most every young platoon leader is faced with a more personal challenge, i.e., progressing in pilot Readiness Levels (RL), from RL3, to RL2, and finally RL1, a full-fledged co-pilot. Inevitably, new platoon leaders do what every new pilot does; they turn their attention to becoming a fully qualified pilot-in-command.

Platoon leaders had additional responsibilities. Unfortunately, helicopters have a lot of moving parts; parts that reach their lifetime and must be replaced for safety reason. They wear and tear from the continuous vibrations, or they simply break.

When one of these events occurs, our crew chiefs coded the aircraft as Non-Mission Capable (NMC) for one of two reasons: Maintenance (NMC-M) or Supply (NMC-S).

Knowing and understanding the difference between these two codes and the follow-on actions required was critical in our effort to maintain 80% readiness rates.

## The Logbook Reconciliation Process

During my first platoon leader role, I remember placing most of my focus on pilot progression and only later learning the difference between NMC-M and NMC-S during my second platoon leader assignment.

As a commander, I wanted to educate my platoon leaders about these details early on. At least twice a week, we would sit down and review logbooks. During these sessions, my three platoon leaders were expected to provide status reports on each of their aircraft.

- If the aircraft was NMC-M, that meant a crew chief needed to do repairs, and it was my platoon leaders' *responsibility* to complete the work with their assigned crew chiefs
- If the aircraft was NMC-S, that meant the crew chief ordered a part. Sometimes, part orders were canceled because of data entry errors. Again, it was my platoon leaders' *responsibility* to resolve any delays

My platoon leaders learned that we would review statuses regularly and it was their job to return our aircraft to operational condition as soon as possible. Most important, they knew that they would be held accountable, as it was *our leadership responsibility* to maintain equipment readiness.

## *Despite delegating authority to my platoon leaders, I maintained overall responsibility.*

### The Development Process

I used these sessions as coaching opportunities and a part of my leadership development process. At first, the platoon leaders made errors. But, like any healthy habit, they learned the causes for delay and took the necessary follow-up actions.

It became a personal challenge for my platoon leaders to answer every question I asked. Before long, they became champs, and I had little more to offer them on this matter, so I shifted my focus to another area I wanted to improve.

Each area served as a building block and became something new that they would handle on their own. This freed me to keep my focus on what was most pressing, or tackle something new.

These coaching sessions empowered my platoon leaders to be increasingly responsible. More important, they shaped my relationships with them, and they helped me shape the environment I wanted to create for the unit. A win-win scenario!

## Keys to Your Leadership Success

- Employees want to feel empowered.

- Help them learn and grow so that they make decisions on their own.

## Business Insights

Make investing time in developing individuals a priority. As each member grows, your performance improves exponentially.

## Building Cohesive Teams

As you develop individual members, the next step is to get everyone to operate as a team. You want to send a clear message about the operating environment you want to create, what we called our command climate.

The best way to establish a fair environment is to make clear how you expect everyone to get along and work together. One way you do this is through your example, how you treat your unsung heroes, a great indicator of how much you value *all of your employees*.

For example, a Special Operations version of the Air Assault scenario I shared occurred on May 1, 2011, during the capture of Osama bin Laden. You might be aware of the Navy SEALs' role in this joint raid. But, have you heard about the unsung heroes from that mission that included 79 people from the Army, Navy, and the Air Force?

## Unsung Heroes

Two MH-60 Blackhawks took off from a base in Afghanistan with teams of Navy SEALs on board. These aircraft flew for 90 minutes, hugging the mountainous terrain to avoid detection. When they arrived at the bin Laden compound in Pakistan, the first helicopter crashed. The SEALs managed to get out safely and conducted their mission.

In the meantime, the second helicopter linked up with a spare helicopter, returning 38 minutes later to pick up the SEALs and the crashed aircrew.

Key Factors:
- A Blackhawk has about 2.5 hours of fuel:
- Ingress Route -- 90 minutes
- Loiter during SEAL mission -- 38 minutes
- Egress Route -- 90 minutes

During the bin Laden raid, reports indicate that they used two MH-47 Chinook helicopters to refuel the MH-60 Blackhawks. This means that instead of external blivets and generators, the fuel handlers rolled hoses out of the back of the Chinooks to refuel the MH-60 Blackhawks on the ground. This also meant finding a safe refueling location and remaining undetected.

**How did our Blackhawks refuel?**

When I flew UH-60 Blackhawk helicopters in Korea, we trained for this type of mission. Unlike the MH-60s, we could not refuel in-flight, so for every one of our weekly missions, we had a tactical refuel team set up operations to keep us flying.

During these missions, our fuel handlers were the first ones in and the last ones out. They arrived prior to attach hoses to rubberized bags of gas (blivets), setup generators, and establish a refuel point so that when the helicopters arrived, they were ready to pump gas.

They did this in every condition, to include the extreme heat or cold. Perhaps the worst conditions were freezing temperatures on cold nights, where they were expected to pump gas while standing under turning rotor blades that produced winds that made a freezing situation worse.

Just like you, we didn't have any unnecessary positions. Our fuel handlers were important, and we treated them as valued members of our team. They were critical to every mission.

I remember my relationship with Sergeant Bey, the leader of our refuel team. It was his team who came to my aid during my time of need (see Chapter 5) and I was very appreciative of how they helped me get through that difficult situation. I'd like to think that they responded so kindly because they were reciprocating how I had treated each of them on a daily basis. Again, a lesson I learned from Mike Pulliam.

## Keys to Your Leadership Success

Individually, everyone wants:
- To be treated with dignity and respect

- The opportunity to learn and grow

Collectively, everyone wants:
- To feel like his or her contributions matter

- To be a part of something greater

## Business Insights

When you treat others well, to include your unsung heroes, you demonstrate that you expect the entire team to treat each other in the same way. This establishes an environment of dignity and respect, increasing cooperation and teamwork among the members while upholding your personal and company values.

### Minimizing Interpersonal Conflict

Of course, every team and every organization must contend with conflict. Whether two individuals or factions within the organization, any time humans are involved, there is a potential for conflict and jockeying for position.

Your team simply wants a fair playing field. When you maintain your values, you are creating that climate, the positive environment everyone wants.

## Interpersonal Conflict

In one situation involving two officers, a young lieutenant came into my office complaining about a colleague, Danny, a captain who was senior to him.)

> Me: Mike, did you speak with Danny about this first?

> Mike: No, sir.

> Me: Why not?

> Mike: I don't know, sir.

> Me: Well, do you think that was fair to Danny? How would you feel if he did the same to you?

> Mike: *(no reply)*

> Me: Let's pretend that you never came in here. You go back and work this out with Danny. If, after you've done your best to work through this together and you can't work it out, then both of you come and see me, together.

Deep down, Mike knew that his actions were neither loyal nor respectful to Danny. However, he exhibited a natural tendency out of alignment with **our culture**, a mistake that many people make, and many leaders allow. They worked things out and that scenario was relatively easy for me to address.

The problem is that all too often, managers feel the need to intervene and play referee. Unfortunately, as soon as you do this, you've opened Pandora's box and you'll have a continual stream of snipes and complaints presented to you. Now, you have become a referee.

## *As a leader, you have more important issues that need your attention.*

### Conflict Can Destroy the Greatest of Teams

The next example involves multiple members of the organization failing to get along, and their overt and covert actions becoming detrimental to performance. My story comes from a team in the National Basketball Association (NBA).

Kareem Abdul-Jabbar was the most dominant player in the 1970s, having won 5 of his 6 Most Valuable Player awards during his first 10 years in the NBA. He was used to winning. In college, during three years with John Wooden and the UCLA Bruins, Kareem's team had an 88-2 record and won three national titles.

But, in the NBA, you need more than a couple of superstars to win championships. After Kareem's first season, the Bucks signed Oscar Robertson, a veteran all-star guard who still has the sixth most assists in NBA history.

In their second year together, the team gelled and they won the championship. But, Kareem had no repeat championships with the Bucks, and was traded to the Los Angeles Lakers.

The Lakers were the franchise with the second most titles in NBA history. Still, even with Kareem on their side, they did not win another championship during his first five years with the team. In 1980, however, a rookie guard named Earvin "Magic" Johnson became the catalyst that propelled Kareem and a team of superstars to win the title.

Human nature rears its head in the NBA too. Superstars have egos, and the Lakers fell short the following season. In the middle of the next season, everything came to a head. Magic wanted to be traded, but the owner fired the coach instead.

After Assistant Coach Pat Riley took the helm and in 1982, the Lakers won the title for the second time in three years. But, the saga wasn't over. Team conflict remained and the 1980s Lakers were a yet to be determined dynasty on the verge of greatness.

In the off-season, Coach Riley made two important decisions. First, he decided that the younger Magic Johnson would be the leader of this team of superstars. And second, perhaps most important, he laid out his conditions for remaining on the team, conditions that he describes in his book, *The Winner Within*. He called these conditions his Core Covenant.

Riley's Core Covenant amounted to a set of values for his team to move forward. He insisted upon cooperation, which meant making their overarching goal of winning a priority.

Nothing unites people more quickly than when they believe that they are pursuing a common goal under conditions perceived to be fair, or, they have a common enemy.

After he shared his values, Coach Riley asked every player whether they were IN or OUT. It was decision time. Every player needed to commit to his vision or he would be traded.

During the eight years prior to Pat Riley as head coach, the Lakers went to the finals once, where they won the championship in 1980. During the next eight years with Riley at the helm, the Lakers were in the finals seven times, winning four championships.

## Keys to Your Leadership Success

- Insist upon a spirit of cooperation; nothing brings people together more quickly than a common goal or enemy.

- As long as you are fair, reasonable, and **maintain your values**, your team will rally behind your cause.

## Business Insights

Whether individuals or teams, people bond when they have a common objective. At times, the obstacle or challenge *may be you*, or one of your policies.

## Why You Want to Act

It's not difficult to be in charge of an organization that is running smoothly. The leadership challenge, however, is when life happens: people who want something more than just a paycheck, employees who fail to cooperate or collaborate for varied reasons, or simply a lack of harmony within your team.

Leadership implies having the capacity to create a positive environment. You must have an ability to develop competent individuals, build cohesive teams, and minimize interpersonal conflict; all are important to achieving alignment.

Think about any successful leader. Most likely, you will think of someone who is able to get everyone to contribute, work together, and succeed. This takes someone who is strong, someone with the presence addressed in Chapter 2. Simply put, these healthy leaders are the ones who build the best teams.

Leadership presence is about your roots, those inner traits that are less obvious on the surface. Instinctively, others know whether you are a person of character, someone who understands human wants and needs, is aware of what motivates, and knows how to inspire others.

This starts with humility, because you realize your own need to develop and grow, and you have a continuous quest for self-improvement. When others see this in you, you set the example, and they want to be like you!

# Instill & Fulfill

## Steps for the *Leader* to Apply

1. **Alignment.** Revisit your long-term goals from Chapter 2.

2. **Find a mentor,** or a coach you admire who can guide you on your leadership journey.

3. **To go deeper, I recommend the following as well:**

   a. Explore your motivators and de-motivators: your strengths, blind spots, and potential weak areas identified in your results from the Values-Index portion of your 3-part ADVanced Insights™ assessment. Tap in to what makes others "tick."

   b. Understand situational leadership. Read *Leadership And The One-Minute Manager*, by Kenneth Blanchard, Patricia Zigarmi, and Drea Zigarmi. When we recognize that everyone has different strengths and weaknesses, we realize that each of us may need to be directed, coached, supported, or merely have responsibilities delegated. This is another must, a quick read!

   c. Read a book about a great team or an organization and what it took for them to achieve greatness. My example was *The Winner Within*, by Pat Riley. Riley emphasized teamwork, team dynamics, and sacrifices players must make along the way as he led the L.A. Lakers basketball team to multiple NBA championships in the 1980s.

# Teamwork Notes

## In the Next Chapter...

...we'll explore the importance of **communication**, moving from a broader organizational **vision**, to creating an **environment** that promotes teamwork and team building, to the fundamental skills and building blocks essential for interacting with individuals.

# Chapter 4

# 4. Relate & Communicate

Just as Coach Riley had to create buy-in in order for the 1980s Los Angeles Lakers to achieve greatness, you have to create buy-in so that you align others to your cause.

## Vision: Sharing Purpose and Intent

Your purpose for communication is to create new or better awareness, to achieve common understanding.

As you move up the management ladder, you'll have much less direct contact with employees. Without this direct contact, you must rely on your leadership team to communicate your message. And, you'll discover your need to communicate with shorter, clearer messages.

A commanding general (CG), as a senior leader, understands these principles. When I led one of 270 Army ROTC leadership development programs for Major General (MG) John T.D. Casey, here is what he had to navigate in order to communicate his vision to us:

- Each ROTC program, or battalion, belonged to one of three regions
- The three geographic regions were broken down into a total of 13 brigades
- Each of the 270 battalions reported to one of the 13 brigades

MG Casey had to communicate his vision to us through his region and brigade commanders. In order to ensure that 270 battalion commanders like me each received the same message and to ensure consistency, he repeated his message at regional conferences and did "spot checks" during various visits with 13 brigades.

In the three years I served under his command, I felt that MG Casey delivered a clear, simple message and he had my buy-in.

For example, he shared how important it was for our future officer corps to be representative of the U.S. population. The problem was that all too often, it was easier for us to recruit the sons and daughters of service men and women.

But, this approach did not reflect our nations' demographics, and we needed to put more effort into approaching all students in our recruiting efforts. I wasn't aware of this bias and hadn't considered this before. His message was simple and clear; he made his point.

Imagine what would happen if your key leaders did not buy-in to your vision. Your message would be lost in translation, open to interpretation, or merely your words retransmitted without communicating your true intent.

When your key leaders understand your purpose, a critical concept that we called the Commander's Intent, they understand your vision, your why. They buy-in and accept your message as if it were their own.

When this happens, your leadership team can carry out what you intended with passion and purpose, and, without your continuous involvement. They can act within the guidelines you've established and boundaries you've set. When your leadership team is aligned with your vision, everyone in your organization will receive the same message.

## Keys to Your Leadership Success

- Buy-in is critical in order to convey a consistent message throughout your organization.

- The more indirect your contact with employees, the clearer you must be with your messages.

## Business Insights

Continually improve your communication skills.

## Learning Together: Cooperating and Collaborating

The most successful organizations are learning organizations, those that provide everyone the opportunity to exchange information in a safe environment. When teams of teams go into execution mode, the only way to assess performance, learn, and grow effectively is when everyone is sharing their insights.

Many organizations use **After Action Reports** to capture lessons learned from a major event or exercise. All too often, however, this approach fails to promote input from those who perform the work, because the feedback goes into a binder of sorts and contributors never know if their input will have an impact on future events.

A better approach is the **After Action Review (AAR),** an interactive learning process in which everyone participates in a live, post-mortem discussion. Not only is it integral for identifying what actions to sustain or improve upon, it is an important part of your team building and leadership development programs.

We used the AAR throughout my Army career, to learn from one another and to hold each other accountable during the next exercise. When I ran my Army ROTC program in Boston, I witnessed how valuable the AAR was to team building and leadership development.

For instance, at the start of each school year we made a special trip, travelling two hours by bus to arrive at the Leadership Reaction Course (LRC) on Cape Cod. The primary purpose of our trip was to give cadets in their junior year an opportunity to practice their leadership skills in a challenging environment. The next summer, they would attend their most important evaluation, the ROTC Advanced Camp.

The LRC had multiple stations in which every cadet had a chance to lead. What the juniors did not realize was that the probability of success at each of these stations was very low. There were never enough resources, but somehow the leader was supposed to find a way to make use of what he or she was given, and then guide their team of 6-7 people to success while overcoming unusual obstacles.

At the end of the allotted time, we conducted an AAR before moving to the next station. After a few rotations and corresponding AARs, everyone began to realize that the purpose of the LRC was more about how they chose to lead than actually succeeding.

As expected, our cadets learned quite a bit about themselves during the AAR, where we encouraged everyone to share observations and provide constructive feedback. You could see a shift in attitude as the day went on, the amount of cooperation, and both the leadership and team building skills our cadets were realizing.

From my career experiences, I knew the value everyone would receive from the feedback, but I had forgotten about the war stories. During the bus ride home, cadets recounted how they would have accomplished the impossible if only given another chance. The common struggle, along with a fair environment to share lessons learned with one another, was an important part of bonding and the team building process.

## Keys to Your Leadership Success

The keys to a successful AAR are the Rules of Engagement (ROE), which typically include:

- Make only constructive comments

- Keep focused on what should be improved or sustained

- Leave your seniority and thin skins at the door

## Business Insights

The most successful organizations are learning organizations. Create a safe environment for open, ongoing dialogue so that everyone feels free to share and contribute to improving your team.

## Communication Skills: Relate and Communicate

We all have our preference or style of communication. There are four basic styles: Decisive, Interactive, Stabilizing, and Cautious.

When you know the four styles and learn how to speak the other person's language, it gives you a distinct advantage in your ability to relate and communicate with others more effectively.

Five years after I was in the Army and had my initial struggles, I reached a point where I was comfortable and confident with my navigation abilities. No sooner than when I achieved that goal, I let my guard down and learned a valuable lesson about communication.

We were on a two-helicopter night vision goggle training flight in South Korea. At the end of a successful exercise, our two aircraft decided to split and return home separately. Because of our choices, we would return first.

We were only 15 miles south of the airfield; I was tired, and ready to call it a day. I set down my map and told my co-pilot to fly north; we'd see the airfield lights in a few minutes. Before I knew it, the other aircraft was landing. We were lost and low on gas. We ended up landing our helicopter in a frozen rice paddy.

Next, I found myself flagging down a taxi so that I could make a phone call that would prevent a less-than-career-enhancing search and rescue operation. When the taxi stopped, my new challenge was that I did not speak Hangul.

After living in South Korea for three years, among the many questions I was asking myself: why didn't I learn the language? I vowed that I would not make the same mistake again.

Years later, I would serve for six months in Honduras. I had taken Spanish in high school and was able to communicate. I made the effort to expand what I knew, which was useful and appreciated by those we worked with in Central America.

A couple of years later, I would be assigned to Germany for three years, but I did not speak the language. This time, I made the effort to learn the language new to me.

After I was in Germany for a year, my parents and brother came to visit, and we took a trip to Bavaria, the southeastern part of Germany. One day, we ended up having a late lunch in a remote area. When the waitress approached, she said in perfect English:

Waitress:    I'm sorry but I don't speak English.

Me (*in German*): *No problem, I speak German. I'll translate for my family.*

Do you think this waitress treated me differently? Of course she did.  Knowing the language made a difference in every interaction I had with German people for the next two years.

The same is true with your employees:
- Do you speak their language?

When you discover the four communication styles and learn to recognize the signals, you simply have to answer these two questions:

- Are they introverted or extroverted?
- Are they people-oriented or task-oriented?

Answering these questions enables you to identify which of four communications styles they prefer to use, and then you'll be able relate and communicate with them by speaking their language.

For example, a salesperson is typically more talkative and expressive, an extrovert.    An accountant may be the opposite, an introvert. Further, a salesperson is likely to be people-oriented, while an accountant is likely to be task-oriented.

## Keys to Your Leadership Success

- We have different communication preferences and we each use one of four styles.

- Know your communication style, the styles of others, and discover how to communicate with each of the four styles.

## Business Insights

Speak the other person's language so that you can relate and communicate more effectively.

### Why You Want to Act

Revisiting the skills curve from the Introduction, effective communication skills are essential for leaders because these "people" skills are your primary interpersonal skills critical to your success.

Whether building relationships and trust, developing individuals and building teams, or sharing your vision with teams of teams, you must become increasingly proficient at communication as you move up the management ladder.

# Relate & Communicate

> ## 68% of recruiters rate communications skills most important.
> ## -- 2014 Bloomberg Poll

## Steps for the *Leader* to Apply

1. **Download my FREE eBook,** *Relate and Communicate: How Leaders Influence, Inspire, and Move People to Action,* to increase your knowledge and understanding of the four communication styles.
http://info.blackhawkleader.com/understanding-disc

2. **For deeper understanding, I recommend:**

   a. Read *How to Win Friends and Influence People,* by Dale Carnegie. This 1936 timeless classic is about building relationships and influencing others. It starts with a focus on personal interaction and being likeable, and then moves into giving criticism and driving improvement, and establishing space for cooperation..

   b. Explore your communication style and preferences identified in your results from the DISC-Index portion of your 3-part ADVanced Insights™ assessment.

## Communication Notes

## In the Next Chapter...

...we'll address how to **refresh the cycle**: deciding whether to **manage or lead**, a process of continuous learning, always returning to your roots, the **values alignment** that will sustain your focus and keep you moving forward.

# Chapter 5

# 5. What's Your Gyroscope?

Most people are aware that a horoscope has to do with astrology, your birthday, and psychic readings that they sometimes use to guide their lives.

Fewer people know that a gyroscope is a critical component of an aircraft navigation system. When it operates as designed, a gyroscope is balanced, stable, and very accurate for navigation and direction. It's like your inner guidance system that serves you so well.

In the last chapter, I shared the story where I got low on gas and we had to land our helicopter in a frozen rice paddy. What I did not reveal was how I got to that unexpected point, the realization of being off-course, or the personal embarrassment the event caused me.

That evening, our two aircraft successfully finished navigating an intense, 90-minute, night, flight training route. At the point where Dan Mangers, the pilot-in-command of the other helicopter, and I decided to part ways for the final leg home, he opted to practice an instrument approach. That meant he would climb and make some additional turns. We should have landed first.

Instead, a couple of signals made me uneasy. First, we crossed a set of streaming white lights heading in one direction, and red lights going the other way. You've seen it as well when you fly at night and pass over a city; these lights are cars on the highways below. In South Korea, there was only one highway like that at the time, and it was a known barrier 15 miles to the east of the airfield.

I double checked our compass and confirmed that we were heading north, so I ignored what I was seeing below.

Next, I heard Dan's calls to the airfield tower. When it became obvious that they were landing before we were, I had an uneasy feeling. I told my co-pilot to climb. Before I knew it, the master caution light starts flashing along with the associated audio blaring, telling us we were low on gas and it was time to land.

After all of the time and effort I put into being better at navigation during the past five years, this was not a welcomed event!

Because of my failure, my crew of three would spend a freezing winter's night in our cold metal helicopter. After getting to a phone, making the necessary call to avoid a search and rescue operation, and coordinating fuel to arrive the next morning, I had time to think about what had gone wrong.

## My gyroscope failed.

Because my gyroscope slowed down from its normal operating speed, it was no longer providing accurate heading information. Instead of heading north as I thought, we were heading east. I failed to recognize the situation.

Just as a helicopter has a gyroscope that is essential to accurate navigation, you have an inner gyroscope that guides you as you navigate life's challenges and your leadership responsibilities.

When your inner gyroscope is aligned and operating at proper speed, you stick to your values, you become efficient at digesting information, and you have the resilience to remain in sync with your values.

Then, you move in the right direction and you make the best decisions possible. By remaining true to your values, you establish who you are, your presence, and exhibit the character (DO) that others expect from you as a leader.

## Servant Leadership (BE)

- What are your reasons for wanting a leadership position?
- What is your purpose: to serve, or to be served?
- Where is your inner gyroscope leading you?

A couple of years ago, I delivered a presentation on Servant Leadership for the Duquesne University's School of Leadership and Professional Advancement as part of their Leadership Breakfast Series.

Selfless service is one of the Army values, so I felt honored to be able to share my experiences and the importance of serving others as a principle for leading. After all, some of the most successful movements in the past century came because a servant led the cause: Mohandas Gandhi, Mother Theresa, and Martin Luther King Jr., to name a few.

During my research, I discovered what Robert Greenleaf had written when he introduced the term servant leadership in his 1970 essay, "The Servant as Leader." His servant leader test:

- Will those served grow as persons?
- Will they, while being served, become healthier, wiser, freer, more autonomous, more likely themselves to become servants?
- What will be the effect on the least privileged in society; will they benefit, or, at least, not be further deprived?

I also reviewed Adam Grant's 2013 book, *Give and Take*, which reinforced Greenleaf's ideas and what I experienced throughout my Army career.

### Keys to Your Leadership Success

- In *Give and Take*, Adam Grant concluded that servant leaders are more highly regarded by their employees, feel better about themselves, and accomplish more.

## Business Insights

Consider Robert Greenleaf's servant leader test and ask yourself his three questions to help you decide your purpose as a leader.

## A Continuous Learning Process (KNOW)

- Are you humble enough to realize that you don't have all of the answers?
- Are you willing, and able, to let others on your team help you find them?
- Where is your inner gyroscope leading you?

Self-awareness and self-improvement are essential ongoing processes not only for every leader, but also for the people you serve. By your learning example, you display humility and make it known that everyone has room for growth, a critical aspect of every learning organization.

---

**"If you seek to lead, invest at least 50 percent of your time leading yourself."**
**-- Dee Hock**

---

## Keys to Your Leadership Success

Continually seek self-improvement by increasing your knowledge of:

- Yourself (self-awareness)

- Technical aspects of your work (technical skills)

- Human interaction aspects of your work (people skills)

## Business Insights

Continuous learning is essential for every leader and another way to set the example, demonstrate humility, and create an environment for everyone to grow.

## Management vs. Leadership (DO)

- What is keeping you on course?
- How will you maintain the culture and values of your organization?
- Where is your inner gyroscope leading you?

In Chapter 1, I shared with you a couple of stories about Mike Pulliam, my first Battalion Commander, the officer I still hold in highest regard after my 20 years of service.

After working for Mike for 23 months, I departed just prior to his change-of-command to attend a couple of Army schools. As fate would have it, seven months later I was back in the same battalion, indirectly working for Mike's successor.

I quickly sensed that the mood was different. The once positive environment had changed and officers no longer felt that they could make mistakes and still feel supported. Morale had decreased and people were less willing to demonstrate initiative or take risk.

For the officers junior to me, their first impressions were much different than mine. I felt badly for them. I wondered whether any were questioning, as I had, whether they were in the right place, or they had made the right career choice.

If I had not worked for Mike first, would I have reached an entirely different conclusion about the Army and its culture?

Let's look at a couple of more definitions:

- Management – to direct or control the use of, to exert control, or to make submissive to one's authority, discipline, or persuasion
- Leadership – to show the way, to guide, or to direct

## Keys to Your Leadership Success

- Management and leadership are both important to your success.

- Lead your people, and manage schedules, tasks, or other things.

- Know the difference between the two.

## Business Insights

You have a big impact on your people and their impressions. Management and leadership are not the same. Semantics to some, but if your people are your most valuable resource, you must demonstrate that you know the difference between managing and leading.

## Why You Want to Act

When I discovered the reason for my demise that my gyroscope failed, causing my aircrew to spend a freezing winter night with me inside a cold metal airframe, I was personally and professionally embarrassed.

I knew that it was my fault and that I would be penalized after we returned home. But, I admitted my mistake and accepted responsibility. To my surprise, I had the support of people like SGT Bey and his refuel team who rescued me the next day, as well as others and throughout my recovery phase the next month.

My failed gyroscope reminded me of several important principles when it comes to your presence, intellect, character, and achieving alignment:

1. Gyroscopes operate within a closed environment. This environment is similar to the boundaries that represent your values, define your culture, and enable you to **(BE)**, your presence.

2. When at operating speed, gyroscopes provide accurate and reliable navigation information. Just as when you are up to speed and you receive the correct input, you have the knowledge you need to make the most informed decision **(KNOW)**.

3. When they maintain their operating speed, gyroscopes are very effective and they act in

the way they are expected: balanced, stable, and providing accurate direction. When you have your momentum, it is much easier to act in a way that reveals the character **(DO)** you want to display most.

## Steps for the *Leader* to Apply

1. **Act.** As part of your lifelong, continuous self-improvement process includes maximizing your long-term efforts. Here are two learning techniques that will help you improve your productivity:

   a. Pomodoro Technique – focus for 25 minutes followed by a 5-minute break; repeat 3 times, then take a longer break. The breaks give you time to recharge, and come back more focused and refreshed. Alternatively, you could focus for 50 minutes and break 10 minutes, OR 75 and 15 minutes, like a college class schedule

   b. Spaced Repetition – This technique is the opposite of cramming. By slowly chipping away at something you are learning, your retention will improve significantly. Check out the video below associated with this graph: https://youtu.be/DcHFq803Tgo

## Spaced Repetition

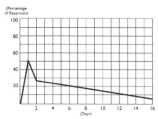

**One exposure to an idea results in only 2% retention after 16 days.**

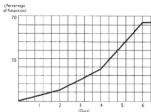

**Six exposures over 6 days results in 62% retention for 15 years.**

*Take off to new possibilities!*

# Continuous Self-Improvement Notes

# Epilogue

Lieutenant General (LTG) William "Gus" Pagonis, Director of Logistics during the Gulf War, was widely recognized for his achievements. In 1991, he was given the responsibility to deploy U.S. Forces to the Gulf for Operation Desert Shield and Operation Desert Storm.

In *Moving Mountains*, Pagonis shares what can happen when your leadership team is aligned. When everyone on the team subscribes to the same set of values and promotes the culture, they work together more effectively and achieve the organization's goals. In this case, literally moving mountains.

Within the first 30 days of Operation Desert Shield, LTG Pagonis and his staff needed to move the equivalent of a city's worth of people and all of their belongings to Saudi Arabia. In the next 60 days, he would have to repeat that same feat a half-dozen times more, only a fraction of the tests that lay ahead of him.

When the team is aligned and guided by the same set of values, great accomplishments like these are possible. Nothing eases effort more than when the employees are aligned with their culture. When leaders inspire trust and confidence, develop individuals and build teams, and communicate their vision and intent clearly, they are the best in their industry.

Finally, use your gyroscope to keep you and your team moving in the right direction, pursuing values-based goals, while you continue to develop your BE-KNOW-DO as someone who wants to be happier, work well with others, and more successful.

# Unleash Your Values

# Suggested Reading

FM 6-22, *Army Leadership*, Red Bike Publishing, 2010

*Give and Take: Why helping Others Drives Our Success*, Adam Grant, Penguin Publishing Group, 2014

*Grounded: How Leaders Stay Rooted in an Uncertain World*, Bob Rosen, Jossey-Bass, 2013

*How to Win Friends and Influence People*, Dale Carnegie, Pocket Books, 1998

*Leadership And The One-Minute Manager*, Kenneth Blanchard, Patricia Zigarmi, and Drea Zigarmi, HarperCollins Publishers, 2000

*Nuts: Southwest Airline's Crazy Recipe for Business and Personal Success*, Kevin & Jackie Freiberg, The Doubleday Religious Publishing Group, 1998

*The One-Minute Manager*, Kenneth Blanchard and Spencer Johnson, HarperCollins Publishers, 2003

*The 7 Habits of Highly Effective People*, Stephen Covey, Simon & Schuster, 2013

*The Winner Within*, Pat Riley, Penguin Publishing Group, 1994

# Keynotes & Leadership Development Seminars

Each chapter in this book serves as the basis for a distinct message Tom delivers in the following keynotes and leadership development seminars:

- **Define & Align: The Leader's Path to Success**

- **Lead & Succeed: How to Earn Trust and Gain Confidence as a Leader**

- **Instill & Fulfill: How to Develop Individuals and Build Teams**

- **Relate & Communicate: How to Influence, Inspire, and Move People to Action**

For customized sessions specific to your audiences' needs, contact tom@blackhawkleader.com and schedule your next speaking engagement.

# Book Tom Crea Today!

# Leadership Development Coaching

For individual or group coaching sessions, contact tom@blackhawkleader.com or visit blackhawkleader.com/leadership-development-coaching/

# Assessments

Individual Orders: visit
blackhawkleader.com/leadership-assessment-tools/

Bulk Orders:  For quantity orders that include consolidated team reports, contact tom@blackhawkleader.com.

# Book Orders

Available from Amazon.com and other online stores.

Bulk Orders: For quantity orders or delivery in coordination with a scheduled speaking engagement, contact tom@blackhawkleader.com.

**NOTE: 10% of all book proceeds support Tom's favorite charity, APUFRAM in Honduras.**

# Connect with Tom

blackhawkleader.com

linkedin.com/in/thomascrea

OR
linkedin.com/company/all-about-leadership

youtube.com/blackhawkcoach

facebook.com/blackhawkcoach

twitter.com/thomascrea

# Disclaimer

The anecdotal stories in this book are based on the author's personal and professional experiences. Any slights of people, places, or organizations are unintentional. There are no quick fix paths to leadership. Your results will depend on how much time and effort you invest. It is your responsibility to apply the information provided in this book and incorporate it into your own life.

# About Tom Crea

Tom Crea encountered leadership unexpectedly. He had a passion for playing basketball, and perhaps like you, someone needed to step up and coordinate getting others involved for weekend games. One leadership role led to the next, and Tom found his passion for serving others.

As an Army officer and Blackhawk helicopter pilot, Tom interacted with soldiers from Private to 4-star General in aviation, information technology, and higher education positions. His diverse responsibilities, along with his frontline, "in the trenches" experiences, involved relating and communicating with a range of people.

Today, Tom keeps audiences on the edge of their seats as he delivers keynote presentations, workshops, and seminars.

Among Tom's interests are cycling, coaching basketball, and supporting his favorite charity, APUFRAM in Honduras.

Tom lives in Pittsburgh, Pennsylvania with his wife Martha and their two sons.

To learn more or to schedule Tom for your next event, visit blackhawkleader.com or you may reach him at tom@blackhawkleader.com